ORDINARY BODIES

ESTEBAN RODRIGUEZ

word west press | new york

copyright © 2022 esteban rodriguez

all rights reserved. no part of this book may be used or reproduced in any manner without written permission from the publisher except in the case of brief quotations embodied in critical articles or reviews. for more information, contact word west press.

isbn: 978-1-7369477-2-2

published by word west in new york

first us edition 2022

printed in the usa

www.wordwest.co

cover photo: esteban rodriguez

cover & interior design: word west

Contents

Inheritance / 9

    I.

Smuggle / 13
Krause Springs / 14
Cleanse / 17
Hard / 18
Curdle / 20
Dress Up / 21
October 13th, 1996 / 22
Somnambulist / 23
Floor / 25
Dealer / 26
Animal Control / 28
Cleanse / 29
Heist / 31
Boujee / 32
Dingleberry / 34
Atonement / 35

    II.
El cuerpo / 37

III.

Displacement / 56
Stench / 57
The Stranger / 59
Lice / 60
Revlon / 62
Ouija / 63
Cleanse / 64
Tattoo / 66
Schlitterbahn / 67
Karaoke / 68
Tap Out / 69
Lost / 70
Repoed / 71
Pedialyte / 72
Roots / 75
Victory / 76

for María Elena and Pedro Espinoza

"The body is the instrument of our hold on the world."
~ Simone de Beauvoir, *The Second Sex*

Inheritance

Not just his shortness, belly,
the silence my father leaned on
at barbecues, birthday parties,
but his white F-150, the hours
he put into it on the weekends,
hoping that if he spent the time,
cared and maintained the engine,
it would start on Monday morning,
and would reassure him that this
was mine to inherit, that if he couldn't
leave me the fluency of his language,
or the experience of having to cross
into a different country, he at least
had this truck, and I had memories
of times he taught me to drive it,
the wide turns, hard brakes, the way
I cursed at the steering wheel,
unsure what it had against me,
or why it was in the way the nights
my father, knowing it was soon
time to let me go, trusted me
to take it out, and I, having sweet-
talked my girl to bring her body near,
had to battle with the wheel,
had to angle myself in positions
my father never had to, since he,
sore and sunburnt after work,
merely sat in the seat, relieved
in ways I was still trying to feel.

I

Smuggle

At some point, your parents must have felt
like you feel now, confined, claustrophobic,
unsure if riding in a trunk was a good idea

after all, although, from what you think you know,
they were not in some friend's car, but
rather packed in the back of a cargo truck

with fifty other women and men, all sweating,
fatigued, unaware how much longer they'd
have to bear the dark, or of what would

happen if they were caught, which for you,
is nothing but in-school suspension, than
a reflection of why you wanted to go to the beach

so bad, but for your parents meant soldiers,
cartels, a coyote warning that if they wanted
to reach the country's edge, they'd have to pay

again, and if not, be left by the side of some
unpaved road, where without any signs, cars,
they'd travel what they think is north, knowing,

from what they've heard, that if they made it
to the other side, the risk would be worth
the reward.

Krause Springs

Then, you slip on a rock.
And though you recover, walk out
and play off your fall with a smile,
laugh, you see that your toe has suffered,
that the nail's been opened, filled
with algae, fresh beads of blood.
And as you imagine amoebas feasting
on this wound, you think of your mother,
her diabetes, the way her feet began
to decay, became dried, bruised,
as black as mold, until one day
she could no longer move,
and bed-bound and less of herself,
had to watch as they got worse,
as her nails looked like yours look now,
broken, without form, tragic in ways
you don't have the language for,
but which you feel when you become
aware you can dig the algae out,
cut off the nail, and not have to worry
if your body has the strength to heal.

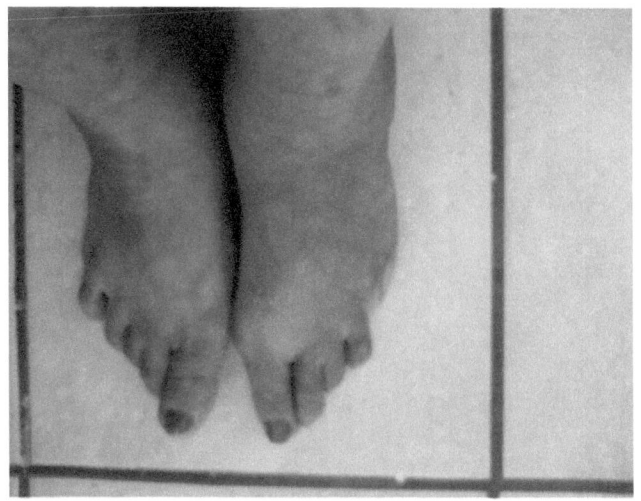

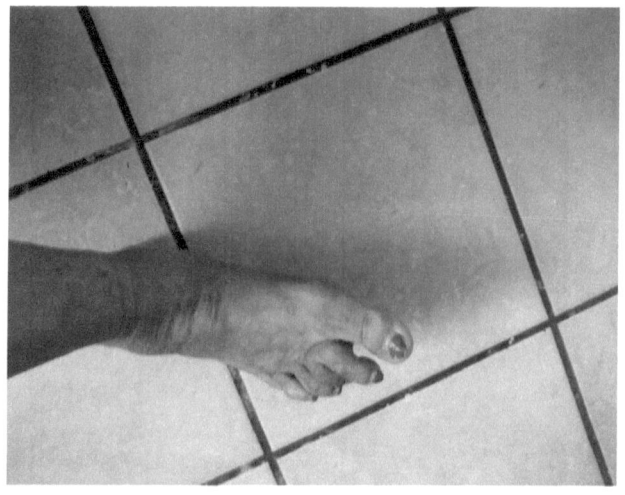

Cleanse

After Dolly downed the clothesline, turned
the ground inside out, my mother dragged me
to the laundromat, where together we stuffed
a washer with dirty clothes, hoping no one
would see our skid marks, soda spills, the grease
unable to love the heat from a frying pan.

There was old blood, dry sweat, pit stains
and blots of piss on underwear we should
have thrown away, but didn't, thinking
that everything could be cleansed, or at least changed,
become as bright pink as the panties I found
when, at home, in charge of folding a load,
I picked them from the pile, knowing
they weren't my mother's, but wishing
they were, and picturing her at night,
when we were all in bed, slipping
into them, ready to feel what felt so right
on someone else's skin.

Hard

With no bathroom for refuge,
no bed and blanket to let friction

play out, I cup my hands together,
push down on my crouch,

pretend, as I stand in line,
watch boy after boy dive,

that I'm cold, that having already
jumped myself, I now have to endure

the air, not let its warm caress
make me feel more aroused.

But oh how I fail, can't stop
myself from being hard, can't stop

thinking, even as I cross my legs,
about the images I think about at night,

about what I once heard a priest say
was wrong, a *disappointment* to be exact,

a pathway to greater sin, a lifestyle
I'd have to cleanse through prayer,

prayer, prayer, or perhaps a baptism,
a body of water like this pool,

which I hope, as I climb the stairs again,
walk toward the end of the board,

will make my body soft, will cause
the hardest parts of me

to either shrink or disappear.

Curdle

In the back of the fridge
lies milk curdled to the gray
embodiment of someone's idea
of death. Half-full, expired,
you already know how it will
smell, and still, you open the lid,
take a whiff, let yourself make
associations—burb, vomit,
animal carcass, the inside
of your grandfather's house,
as well as your grandfather's skin;
the stench it emits, the way
it confesses his body had given up,
that although he still has form,
occupies space, purpose is no longer
in play, and that like this gallon
of milk you smell once again,
serves only to remind you
what little time you have left.

Dress Up

First, eyeshadow, lipstick,
the powdery stuff your mother
rarely uses. Then, with your face
brightened, gaze softened,
rummage your mother's closet,
exhume dresses that no longer fit,
and one by one, like you imagine
models do, try each on, convinced
this is all in jest, that you don't like
the flower-patterned fabric,
nor the way it feels against your skin.
No, you tell yourself. *Fuck no.*
This is all a prank. But because it is,
you must go through with it, strut back
and forth and back, giggle, laugh,
embody every synonym that best
describes how you look at yourself
in the mirror, toss your imaginary hair
back, and with a smile that's both coy
and confident, believe you're not just
beautiful, but different.

October 31st, 1996

The year there was no makeup, masks, no old
costume that would welcome your body back,
or no language for irony, indifference, for
telling people that everything about Halloween
was bullshit, you cut a hole in a black trash bag,
put it on, and without waiting for someone
to ask you what you were, you said Death,
the King of Ruin, the one who gives Satan
a run for his money, that invisible figure lurking
on every street corner, waiting for the slightest
accident: hit-and-run, red light ran, a power line
that suddenly snaps, electrocutes the most
innocent of pedestrians. Yes, you were
the Taker of Life, and as you went from house
to house, opened your candy bag, you thought
the sweets you were given were given out of fear,
and not, as you now look back, out of guilt,
obligation, out of knowing that no matter
how much you receive, anything at any moment
can be taken.

Somnambulist

There were nights my mother rose
from bed, walked half-clothed and barefoot
to the kitchen, and instead of letting loose,

mixing orange juice with those bottles
of tequila on the fridge, she'd wash dishes
that were already washed, rearrange the spices

in the cabinets, clean the microwave, stove,
and if my father hadn't already shrugged
her awake, brought her back to bed, she'd sit

at the table, raise an invisible glass,
and toast everything she'd done that day:
dusting, laundry, the dinner neither my father

nor I finished, but which we said we liked,
even if we knew she knew we didn't.
Yes, on nights I watched this, she'd toast

herself again, again, and mumble, in between
her smiles, laughs, what I thought was
a *Buen trabajo, Maria. Good job*,

because who else was going to say it,
who but her would make sure
her work didn't go unnoticed?

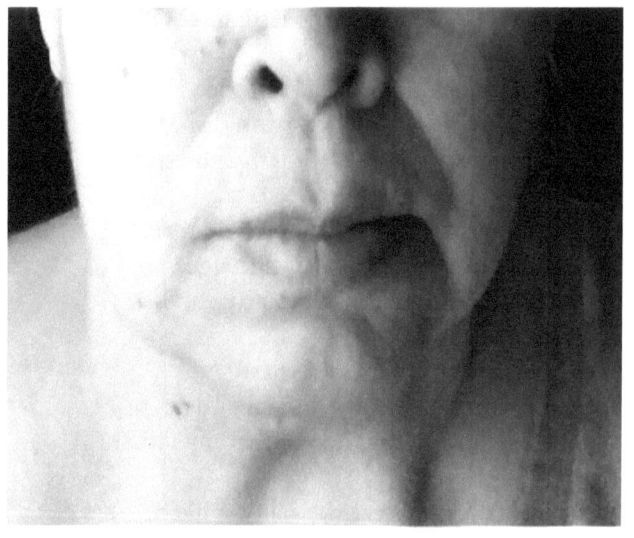

Floor

This time, you walk through it,
unaware that it was just mopped,
that the custodian, standing a few
feet off, is eyeing you, damning
your presence with a stare she maintains
even as you turn, take in the details of her
face, the long winkles, brown complexion,
the raised eyebrows that say you just
ruined her work, that your shoes, stained
with years of ground beneath them,
have added levels of filth to this clean floor.
And though you forget, momentarily,
where you are—hotel, school, your
apartment's lobby—you can't help but think
of your mother, of how she bites her tongue
like this lady does, and always looks like she
wants to shout, curse, ask if there is anything
in that hallow head of yours. And even if
she doesn't, you start to pretend you weigh
nothing, and hear the disappointment
in her silence, the acknowledgement
that in this world there are some jobs
that are never finished.

Dealer

Like ornaments, they hung,
pairs of shoes that from where

I stood, looked as if they
were barely worn, as if their

placement on power lines
had been a prank, or revenge

for something petty, for what
could only be righted by being

thrown. So, to protest the shoes
I didn't want, but which my parents

still bought, I tied these not-Js
together, threw them as high

as I could, and with pride, a sense I
had shown *the man*—whoever he was—

who was really boss, I confessed
my anarchy to anyone near:

cousins, friends, the boy in class
I barely knew, but who, like everyone

else, shook his head, laughed,
saying someone probably saw me,

and that because they had, I'd be
thought of as the new dealer

on the block, and like my parents,
be expected to provide not just

for needs, but wants.

Animal Control

On days it came, I stood outside,
watched a man get off, sigh and look
around, exhume tools from the back

of his truck, and like someone who hates
his job, slumber through the block, scan
halfheartedly yard after yard after yard,

until he found a dog, and seeing that it
had no collar, tag, that it looked like it
had never seen the inside of a house, he

crouched, stuck his pole out, moved
slowly toward his catch, like me on days
I tried to feed the strays, hoping they

wouldn't turn away when I crawled beneath
the porch, and that in the shuffled haze
of darkness, dirt, they'd accept the scraps

I offered them, that like God revealing
himself to his chosen ones, they'd rush up,
eat the feast right off my palms.

Cleanse

Summer, and this much was true:
a horde of stray mutts sprawled
along the fence; cane smoke rising like
a warning from our neighbor's field; my
mother stretching bedsheets, pillowslips,
her figure shaped into a soaked silhouette.
She hangs her last load, ambles
with her basket back inside the house,
and I step into the echo of her shadow,
tug down a line, exhume a Barbie doll
from my pocket, and tie her tangled hair
between a pair of underwear and socks.
I step back, watch the doll twist, twirl,
move with the same randomness
as all my shirts, and as the wind dies down,
and her naked body stills, I wonder if, as my
grandmother claims when my mother scans
the washers at Sears, the clothesline does
indeed have the power to heal, or at least
cleanse the week's stains, smells, remove that
which without a hard scrub and fresh air, will
never disappear. Because Abuela has her own
cures—prayer candles on the stove top, cold eggs
on fevered skin—I trust the line will erase
the way in which, kneeling in the middle
of my sister's room, I took off Barbie's shirt,
puzzled as to what lied beneath, if parts of her
were as different as I had suspected them

to be, and if running my fingers across
her limbs, as my cousins swore they had done
too, would make me feel like someone else,
not the boy who rinsed her plastic body, hung
it on the line, and waited till—like his
mother's nightgown, or his father's work jeans—
it looked as untouched as it did when it was
still new.

Heist

Already I see myself tearing
the backside open, releasing Billy
from his plastic prison. And with
the package in my hand, and the aisle's
camera on the opposite end, I know
I can get away with this, that if
I stuff this action figure in my pocket,
pretend nothing happened, I will walk
right out, a Power Ranger richer.
But I freeze, begin to play potential
movie scenes: alarms going off,
gates closing, the golf cart-cruising cop
in the parking lot chasing me down.
And I wonder how my mother once—
that day at the end of the month—
could have looked at a chocolate bar,
and without a second thought slipped it
in her purse, perhaps because the dollar
it cost wasn't in the budget, and she knew
that if you wanted what you wanted,
the punishment would be worth
the reward.

Boujee

Short for popped collars, UGGs,
ripped jeans, for cheerleaders,
jocks, for teachers who spoke

like they were never from
the same neighborhood as us,
for needing to believe,

because I was in a group
that wasn't a part of the group,
that I didn't want American Eagle

gear, seashell necklaces, shirts
that appeared to be doused in bleach,
and the confidence to wear

what was always beyond my parent's
reach, out of league for a father
who worked construction,

for a mother who stayed at home,
would clean a house that was
already clean, for the desire

of wanting what you knew
no paycheck could offer,
and for knowing that even if

you got a Razor, highlights,
colored braces to fix your slightly
crooked teeth, you would still

want more, would wish for things
you wouldn't know how to keep.

Dingleberry

After *douchebag, dumbass, dick*,
it was *dingleberry*, not as heavy, harsh,
but sharp enough to express to the boy
you hurled it at that he was dumb
as shit. And of course, it was boys
you reserved it for, your enemies
as much as your friends, until you saw
your mother come out of the bathroom
once, toilet paper peeking out from
her waist, and knew, right there and then,
how quickly meanings can shift,
that the *dingleberry* you began thinking of
meant crap still clinging to ass,
that she wasn't stupid, but careless,
as unaware as she'd be decades later,
when on the toilet, crying and incoherent,
you pushed her forward, wiped the shit
smeared on her crack, knowing that if
you ever had to retell this, you'd use
the phrase *shit smeared on her crack*,
because the description fit, because
what else would capture how you wiped
and mumbled *dingleberry* to yourself,
so full of uncertainty, so full of regret?

Atonement

Because biology is not my subject,
I fear the wart on my palm,
believe that because I've never

touched a frog, this is likely, as boys
have already claimed, an STD, or AIDS
perhaps, or some other acronym I got

from the night I spent at my friend's
house, and in his bed, after one thing
led to the next, I touched his crotch,

rubbed and rubbed till it became wet.
And because neither God nor the body
ever forget, I now have a wart I pick at,

scratch, try to remove with scissors,
paper clips, with half-hearted prayers
in between each class, so no one sees

and thinks I'm different, so that when I
hand papers back, they don't flinch,
or don't pretend they didn't see

what they just saw, didn't glimpse
at the lump I sometimes pierce
with a pen, as though this time around

it will cure the past, erase
even my most well-kept sin.

II

El cuerpo

Hand

The one that once, in the heat of an argument,
he raised at your mother, and knowing
the history of its power, let it linger above him.
And you wonder what it meant when that hand
rested on your shoulder, heavy and weighted
with burdens you never understood, because really,
what did you know, what hammers had you lifted,
what 2x4s had you sawed, what ground did you claw
to escape the river's greed, and what son had you held
when he was first born, repeating to yourself,
because his skin was soft and new,
Please don't end up like me. Please
don't end up like me. Please
don't end up like me.

Forearm

Here a tattoo. An eagle perhaps,
or some exotic bird, or, when you know
there's no way it's a penguin
or ostrich, you guess a Phoenix,
inked on him after sneaking in
to this side of earth, because
what better symbol than a symbol
of rebirth, than myth on embodied flesh,
than a reminder of how he shed
the river from his skin, climbed
the bank, and though weakened
and out of breath, staggered across
this new land, where years later,
he'd walk into a tattoo shop, ask
for this fiery bird. But because you know
this last part is probably not true,
that your father, even after tossing back
a few, won't answer anything about his past,
you prefer this version to the truth,
to your father having had this piece done
when he was young, unaware that the body—
his body—could be renewed.

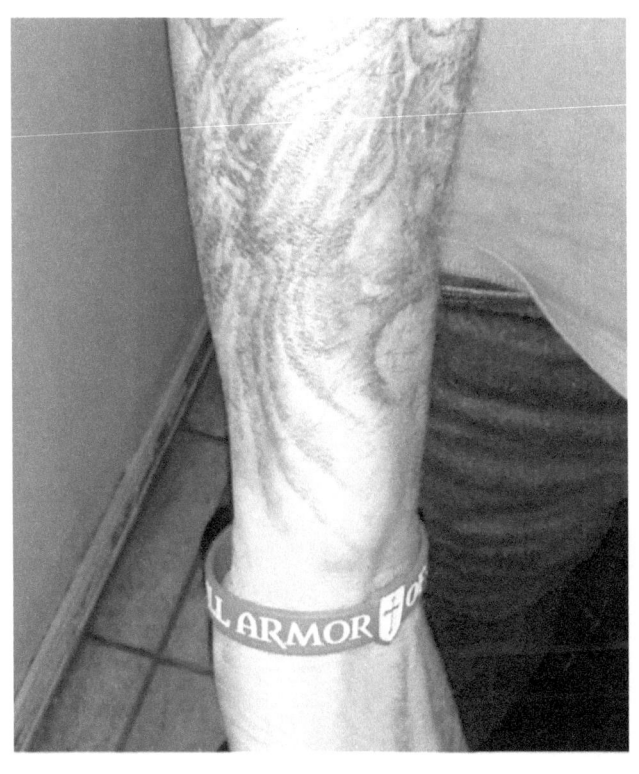

Lips

For context, say thin, chapped,
say as dry as a desert floor,
and just as cracked. Say thirst,
but the kind not even air will touch.
Then imagine silence, a dinner table,
you, your mother, and your father wiping
his mouth with the back of his hand,
saying, without so much as saying
a word, that the food is cold,
doesn't have enough salt,
that he swears if he has to eat
this shit again, he will blow
his brains out. Give him a voice
that sounds and doesn't sound
like yours, because with how little
he talks, you must fill in the gap,
add language where you hear,
day after day, nothing at all.

Legs

Lighter than this arms, neck,
than the face that battles—
three decades and counting—
the daily onslaught of sun,
that army of rays that no matter
what bandanas he uses
to cover up, still lashes
at his skin, makes it look
like aged leather, or like the flesh
of a fresh carcass, or as dark
as any comparison you make
when proximity is no longer
a myth, and you can study him,
take in his face, neck, take in
the legs that, hidden behind
jeans all day, never spar
with the sun, but which you guess
will be, once his body
has clocked out, another thing
no one can say they admired,
loved.

Neck

Seared. No, *scalded, singed.* No,
say something in Spanish, a word
that will prompt your father to rub
the back of his neck, shift in place,
clear this throat and respond, as he responds
to all things that make him reflect,
by walking away. And when he walks away,
feel the word on your skin, feel the sun,
personified—because in what other way
should it exist?—scratch at you, again, again,
until you understand, if only for a moment,
what it means to look like your father,
how a complexion burdened with work
can ache this much, feel almost like sin.

Belly

When he'd come home,
a twelve-hour shift steaming off
his skin, he'd peel off his work shirt,
wife beater, then, after he tossed
his belt and boots like trash
on the floor, he'd unbutton his jeans,
let his starved and hairy gut
hang loose, breathe. And if,
as became the norm year after year,
he had dinner on the couch,
I'd watch how he ate from the plate,
how the plate balanced on his belly,
how, even slouched, he'd guide
every piece of food perfectly
into his mouth, and how with each
bite and chew, he became a cliché
of a father who wanted to just be,
to rest, eat, to forget that tomorrow
when he woke up, got dressed,
the day would be ready to tear down
his body again.

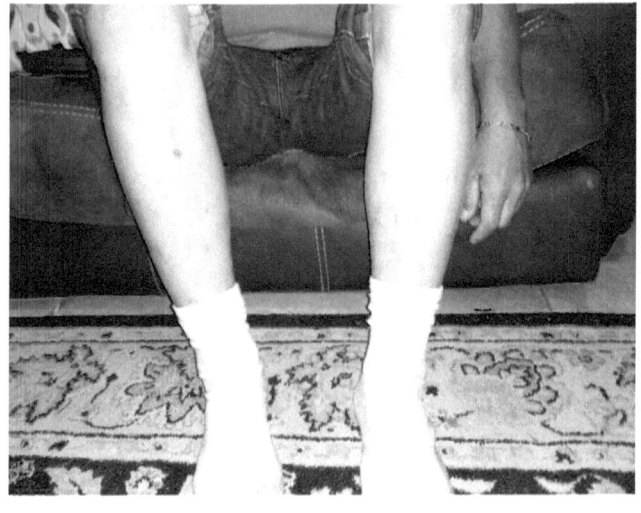

Head

His hair began to disappear,
then his scalp, a new victim
to sunlight, was constellated with
spots I couldn't name: *Bruises*
perhaps? Maybe *moles?* Maybe
*broken blood vessels shaped
like carpet stains?* Or maybe,
if his week was rough,
and he plopped himself for hours
on the couch, I'd say, just
to have a name, that the spots
were *cancer*, that this most random
part of him had been betrayed,
and that soon, after pills
and radiation broke his body down,
I'd no longer recognize his face,
would see a man too on the brink
of death to remember the son
he had, a boy who watched him
unwind every night on the couch,
unsure if the silence he grew to love
was something he'd ever understand.

Knee

It was a valley of spider veins,
a geography I wanted to touch,
run my fingers across, and claim,
if only to myself, that the body too
could be a country. And I wondered
how traveled my mother's was,
if she'd been experienced in the most
random of places: elbows, knees,
the space between her fingers,
toes, the calloused bottoms of her feet.
What about her hips, thighs, the tension
in her shoulders when she saw something
wasn't clean? And what about if I too
had to inherit a landscape like this,
had to accept that every visit
would always feel so brief.

Ankles

Before her ankles, study her toes,
note how, for lack of a better term,
tragic they appear—the big ones
crooked, retired from symmetry,
and no longer persuaded by the cream
your mother makes you rub on them,
nor the pressure you use, nor the saliva-
sprinkled spite you shower them with,
hoping, with each curse beneath your breath,
that they'd turn back to the way they were—
no dead and dry skin, no lumps and spots
you never found the words for.

Lips

One day you notice her mustache,
and apart from not knowing how long
it's been there, or why it still is, you wonder
how your father feels, if he thinks when he
kisses her—if kissing is still something he does—
that she no longer cares, that this alone
makes her less of the woman he thought
he'd always love. Or when he looks at it,
really looks at that light layer of hair,
does he not think this at all, but instead
sees a woman—after all these years—
coming to terms with herself, accepting
what had always been there, but which
she denied her flesh, choosing, because
she had no choice, to shave it off,
or to pluck whatever curls flared from
the corners of her lips, which you imagine
from now on when she kisses you before bed,
will scratch your cheeks, leave you wishing
you felt something more than an itch.

Hands

And so, at night you enter
the kitchen, and half-asleep,
half-sure if this is a good idea,
you turn on the stove, place
the pan on the grate, and when
it's hot enough to feel the heat
on your face, you slap your hand
in the center, see how long
you can take the pain. One second.
Two. And at three you think
of your mother's hands, remember
why you're doing this, remember
every time she stood here,
labored over dinners neither you
nor your father finished, ready,
as always, to ditch the plate
for the couch, TV, for a night
locked away in a separate room,
and, at least for you, for not seeing
your mother's hands when she ate—
no calloused fingers so close
to her mouth, no fresh burns
you could only imagine ached.

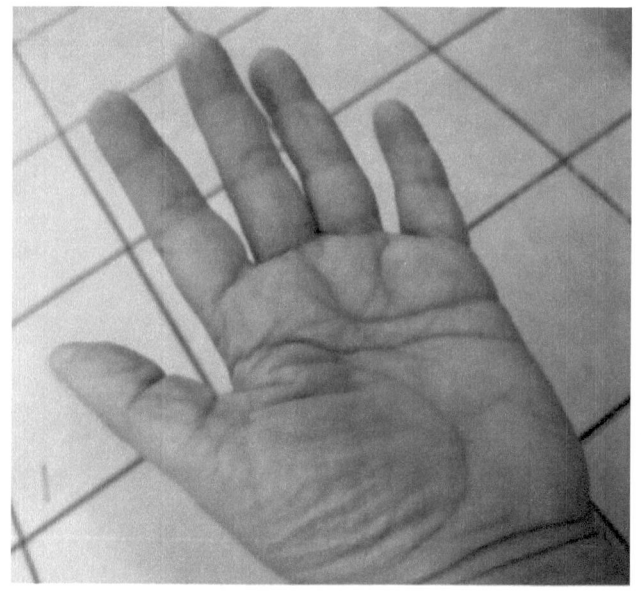

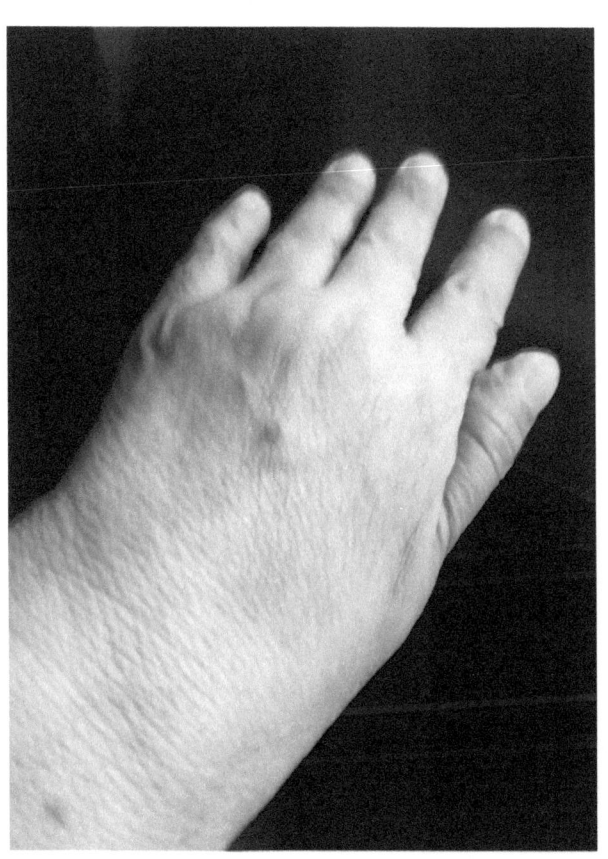

Thighs

Nights my father wasn't home,
she'd rest in his spot, become
according to the phrases I had
just leaned, a *couch potato, bum*,
an *old fart without a damn thing
to do*, only sit and watch a marathon
of *novelas*, or, if she wanted to test
what little English she knew,
watch a sitcom, game show,
anything where she could stretch
her body out, not worry about
how far the bottom of her nightgown
rode up, or that her thighs, webbed
in spider veins and cellulite,
were as exposed as they were,
waiting to be discovered,
touched.

Neck

But why not believe her skin tags
were ticks, that the ones that constellated
her neck were sucking every bit
of life away, that they were to blame
for how tired she always felt,
for spending whole nights on the couch,
days locked in another room by herself,
or for the silence I could hear
throughout the house, asking
what she did to be spited with thick hair,
or with a neck that year after year
looked like it was being fed on.
And those evenings when her silence
grew so loud, I heard it say that she longed
for hands to massage her neck, ease
the loneliness out, and to make her feel
like she deserved this, that for once
her body was seen and thought of
as enough.

Forearm

Days later, and the bruise
looked like a tattoo, a purple tribal
designed so boldly on purpose, so that I,
or anyone who happened to see it,
would know her past was a part
of her present. And when the moment
ended, and I could see the aftermath
of your father's fingers, I moved in
closer, sure that even though my mother
pulled away, she wanted me to notice,
to absorb this slow attempt at closure,
how nothing forced upon her really lasted,
because, as I could hear her say
whenever she reclaimed religion,
the body was but a vessel, a means
to bear the pain we pray becomes
next life's pleasures.

III

Displacement

From the frontage road,
I spot the cardboard, tents,
the overstuffed suitcases
layered with years of dust
and neglect. And as I drive
past this scene beneath the bridge,
I wonder to what extent
my parents once lived like this,
if when they decided to join
the exodus, they filled every inch
of their backpacks with clothes,
aware that as they trekked across
half of Mexico, what they had
was all they had, and they'd have
no choice but to reuse the sweaty
shirts, pants, the underwear
I'm sure my father turned
inside out, the bras my mother,
at night in the back of some truck,
tried to forget about, as if forgetting
would erase the stench, or would ease
the terrain her body felt. There
were the socks that quickly tore,
shoes that ripped, lost their grip,
and there must have been, as I imagine
my parents trudging a dry and rugged
land, rags they wiped their foreheads
with, expecting, this time around,
that when they cleaned the sweat,
the river rising in front of them
wasn't a mirage.

Stench

When the stench grows, I bury
my head between my bicep
and shoulder, pretend that my nose
has an itch, and that if I happen
to take a whiff of my armpit, it is
only by accident. But oh how I know
nothing about this is an accident,
how after morning practice I skip
the shower, put on layers of deodorant,
douse myself in body spray, hoping
that the hours in which I scarified
my body will be erased, and I won't
smell like my father, who, home
from a half-day shift, plops on the couch
reeking of wet cement, or sometimes
of wood, rebar, sawdust and nails,
or sometimes of the river from which
he emerged decades ago. And though
I know nothing of the river or of how
it smells, I imagine that it clings to flesh
for years, and that what I'm smelling
when he walks through the door
is the memory of his crossing,
the struggle to stay afloat, to move
arm in front of arm, again and again,
so that when he reaches the bank,
nearly defeated and soaked, he can
lay down, rest, inhale the fresh air
on this side of earth.

The Stranger

When it came to lust,
you masturbated quickly,
thought of models, actresses,

made up moments where you,
for once, were rounding
all the bases smoothly.

But when you wanted affection,
needed to feel less like the star
of a one-act play, you sat

on your arm, waited for numbness
to kick in, and when it was purple,
swollen, you pretended, the best

you could, that your hand
was actually a woman's—
older, experienced, ready

to teach you things you were too
shy to even say. And so, stroke
after stroke, you watched, learned,

and when the numbness began
to fade, and the guilt resurfaced—
made your whole body shake—

you quickened the pace, hopeful
that when the time came,
you'd no longer feel

you were at this alone.

Lice

Three days in, and my mother
had yet to shave my head,
to caution my uncles, aunts,

to blame my school, claim
they were spreading what might
as well have been the plague.

And because there was no shock,
panic, no long looks of disgust
on my mother's face, I believed

she was hoping that my lice
would spread, that she'd feel
that itch, begin to scratch,

that she'd have no choice
but to cut her hair, snip until
she almost looked bald,

and with this clean slate,
pray that her waves came out
straight, that her bangs wouldn't

be as thin, that she could play around
with what was too often pulled
into a sloppy ponytail, or left

to look like she'd been lost
for days, and after finding her way
home, had whatever answer told her

to look in the mirror, to see herself
as someone new.

Revlon

Un rayo, she joked, *un rayo
kissed my head*. And though
I wanted to laugh, wanted to believe
in the mythology of lightning,
the possibility that a god had chosen
to strike her body, I couldn't,
not when the word *deflection*
was a part of my vocabulary,
not when my mother, in front
of the bathroom mirror, opened
a box, put plastic gloves on,
and like a child gluing together
something they'd broken,
began coloring her hair, scraping
the tip of the bottle against her scalp,
until the bottle was empty
and all she could do was rub,
rub, rub, expecting, it seemed,
that her hair would change instantly,
that after she washed it, let it dry,
she would be a different person,
would see a woman who reversed
the natural course of life.

Ouija

Though you know you alone
control it, you watch the planchette
move, spell out SIN, MASTURBATION,
REPENT when you ask what you
can do to be a better person. And when
you're done asking about yourself,
see the responses you've seen before,
you pretend your parents are dead,
ask them what it's like in the great
unknown, if your mother is no longer
burdened with cleaning a house,
if your father has softer skin,
no leather-like thickness from
working a lifetime in the sun.
And you ask, knowing the answer,
if they no longer feel the aches
in their bones, or no longer have
the memory of crossing into another
land, praying night would be the perfect
accomplice, and that the river,
that ancient antagonist, wouldn't pull
them under, or tug them back to where
they started, and to where they,
soaked and exhausted, could only look
up at the sky, ask a god no longer there,
Why? Why? Why?

Cleanse

No matter how hard you scrubbed,
poured every color of dish soap on a spot,

you still saw your socks as stained,
ruined, once again, by what your body

could no longer keep backed up.
And though you knew that not even

the faintest outline remained, you thought
your mother could still see it, that when

she rummaged the basket for your wet socks,
strung pair after pair on a clothesline wire,

she had a clear image of what you did
in your room, saw how you lied on your bed

in the dark, and how with such passion
you never showed anyone else, you began

to touch yourself, used a sock to cover
the aftermath up, never once thinking,

even when you washed the stains out,
of how long and hard your father worked

to buy your clothes, or of how your mother
spent Sunday afternoons washing and drying

every load, so that on Monday morning,
when you got ready for school, you could start

the week feeling so clean, so new.

Tattoo

Below her clavicle: a heart—
watermelon pink, two dimensional,
pierced by an arrow that was once

bright, bold, that stood for something
I'm sure my aunt no longer remembers,
but which she still likes to flaunt, expose,

draw what attention she can to her chest.
And of course, I look, stare first at the stretch
marks between her breasts, then at this tattoo.

And as I wonder why she chose it,
whether she lacked inhibition, my aunt
catches me staring, and before scoffing,

turning away, she grins, nods, acknowledges
that I acknowledge she was once young,
that she, in love with clichés, thought

of her skin as a canvas, and still does
enough to know that because she's not
famous, has no following to her name,

nothing on or about her body
will endure what time intends to erase.

Schlitterbahn

July. And because the heat has seeped
inside, silenced the A/C's hum, my mother,
the closest thing to God in human form,
casts us to the lawn, where my father sits
shirtless on a folding chair, downing tall boys,
waving at passing cars, and watching,
because watching is what he does on his days
off, my mother rinse the pool—that blue
plastic thing speckled with grime, dead insects,
with spider webs no amount of water can wash
off. And why should my mother care?
Why should I complain when the pool,
murky yet filled, is cool enough to jump in,
to pretend, if just for an afternoon, that
we really didn't want to go to Schlitterbahn,
that waiting in line for hours for such short rides
wouldn't have compared to how relaxed
my father now feels, or to how my mother dips
her toes in the pool, or to the way I begin
to smack the water, splash them both,
sure that as they wave their arms, curse me out,
this is what it looks like to enjoy ourselves.

Karaoke

If they'd karaoke at barbecues,
or at a restaurant, or a birthday party
they dragged you to, they began belting
out fragments of a song without music,
microphones, without a screen flashing
instructions, lyrics. If lucky, you didn't
have to see your parents sing in public,
just the backyard, celebrating, with your aunts
and uncles, the weekly holiday of Saturday,
the fact that they would have Sunday
to recover, and that they could buffer
their headaches and hangovers before work
on Monday, before a construction site
muted the music of your father's body,
before a list of chores cut short the melody
of your mother's movement. If lucky,
you forgot about past embarrassments,
and your parents, as night aged and stars
became blurry, would appear younger,
confident in ways other parents embodied,
and sure that the songs they shouted drunkenly
were meant to reveal what their silence
already said was written for them.

Tap Out

It was pain we wanted,
and pain we found
in every eye-poke,
drop-kick, head-butt,
in the body slams
we perfected in our backyards,
in the way we held
each other in a neck lock,
gripped our forearms
with our hands, and waited
for the sign that said—
at least for this round—
you were not a man,
or not man enough to endure
the grip till you passed out,
to show the boys cheering
your opponent on
that your purple face
was just a phase, and that you,
once all was said and done,
would come out stronger
than before, even if this
was just wrestling, and even if
you knew that pain, in all
its forms, was a lesson
you still had yet to learn.

Lost

Again, they take your Js,
leave a pair of flip-flops
in their place, and as you begin
to search, in just a towel,
the most unlit corners
of the locker room, you think
of your father, how you once saw
him step out of the shower,
so naked, so wet, shaking
like he feared the water,
or as if he remembered how
he crossed the Rio Grande,
aware, each time, that his body
would think of his crossing
not as renewal, but as a trail,
test, as a stretch of endurance
he wasn't guaranteed to pass,
and which he'd come out of,
if he came out of it at all.

Repoed

At night, your father's truck
is taken, and in the morning,
he stands in a truckless driveway,

reflects in silence, nods at
the horizon, as if he believes
that despite its emptiness,

it will acknowledge how unfair
the past few months have been,
that contracts have come and gone,

that rain, a miracle for some,
has docked its share of numbers
off his checks, left him unsure

how to play accountant, or how
to tell your mother that this month
he'd be short, and we'd have no choice

but to cut back, skip aisles at the store,
put $5.87 of gas, search the pantry
for packages, cans, aware that as you all

sit for dinner, scrape the leftovers
from your plates, your family was sure
to lose more, to no longer have

what couldn't be replaced.

Pedialyte

Again, Sprite fails.
And when Gatorade does too,
and my father can barely make it
to the bathroom, my mother,
like a bartender, serves him rounds
of Pedialyte, which my father,
sprawled on the hallway floor,
doesn't refuse, slurring *Más, María,
more... more.* And how could
my mother stop, how could she not
believe, as she poured the liquid
in a cup, that if given enough,
my father, in the morning,
would be free of fever, coughing,
snot, of an illness that if he didn't
get over, would cost him a day of work,
which meant a chunk of paycheck gone,
which meant a bill they couldn't pay,
and which meant, most of all,
that my mother's worst fears
would come true: my father
would have to stay home all day,
and she, like the only version
of a wife she ever knew,
would have to be by his side,
not rest till she found a cure.

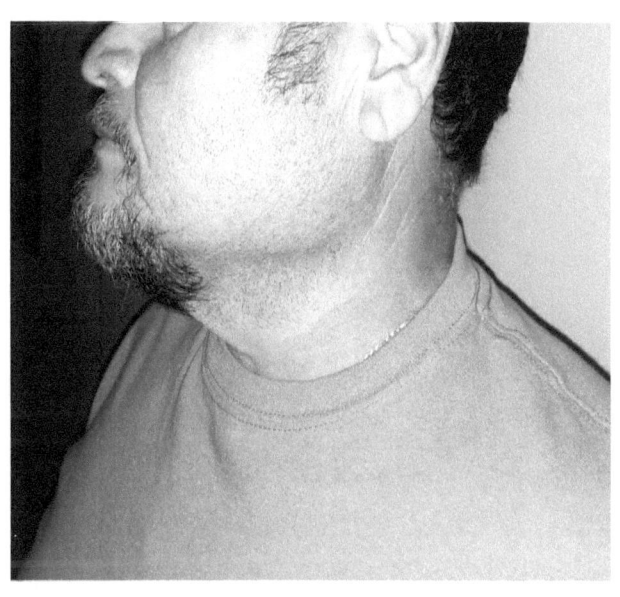

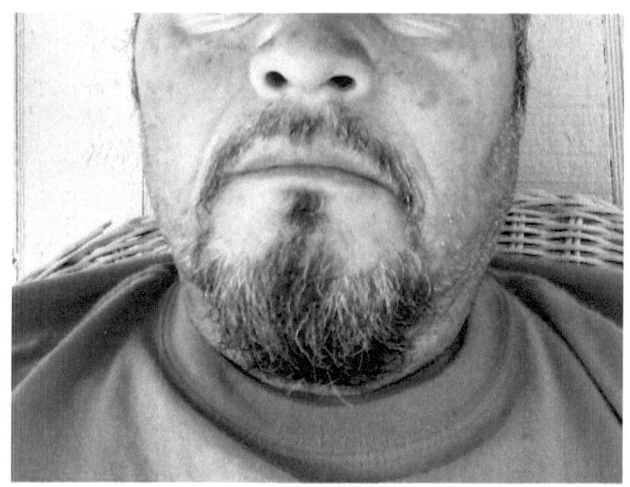

Roots

With his papers in limbo,
he turned toward prayer,
knowing that no matter how much
he kneeled, recited Our Father's,
Hail Mary's, only my mother
could make him feel better.
And so, when she got him to accept
how risky it was to go to Mexico,
she sat him at the kitchen table,
demanded I hold his head,
and with the same pliers my father
used for home projects he never
finished, griped his molar, yanked,
yanked, yanked, unconcerned with
the blood coming out, or with the violent
jerks, shouts, or with—when she finally
pulled the tooth from his mouth—
how rotten even the roots had become,
so jagged, so black, and a reminder
that despite the stability our bodies
want, things never stay as they are.

Victory

Still, I can only guess this
is the way it felt, that that duck
my cousin shot summers ago
experienced each BB as fire, flame,
as every synonym for the burning
I now feel on top of my foot,
this new hole filling with blood
gushing onto my toes, nails.
Maybe the duck too felt the ground
warm, and maybe, when it began
to panic, it thought of its own version
of death, of what could have done
this to its body, of why it was shaking,
giving into its weight. And though
I can only guess what images
we're playing in its head, I play
the moments that led to my fall:
June, BB gun, a backyard I tread
barefoot, pretending I'm on the hunt,
that those birds on the power line
are decoys or spies, that the piles
of leaves are booby traps, or that
the anthill by my feet will,
if stepped on, explode, which is why
I had to shoot it, and why, in my
eagerness for invented victories,
I grew careless, fired at myself,
and am now writhing on the ground,
trying not to go toward the light,
but wishing, like I wished
for that duck, that if my body
is found, it will least look
like I put up a fight.

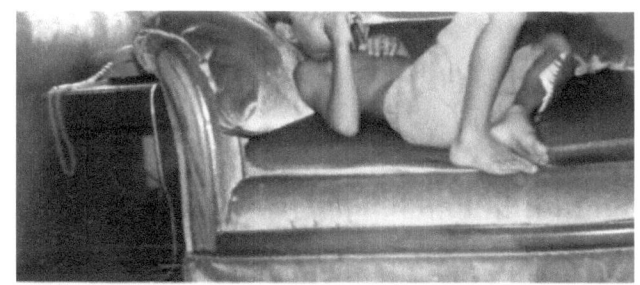

ACKNOWLEDGMENTS

Many thanks to the editors of the following magazines and journals in which some of these poems first appeared:

> *Cortland Review*: "Cleanse"
> *Latino Book Review*: "Somnambulist"
> *Parhelion Literary Magazine*: "Smuggle"
> *Passenger Journal*: "Atonement" and "Displacement"

Special thank you to my mother, sister, and father for the photographs included in this collection.